Woodcut by Vasyl Lopata

The Kozaky Re-enactors Handbook

GW01459067

Woodcut by Vasyl Lopata

A guide to recreating a mid-seventeenth century Ukrainian Kozak (Cossack) character

DEDICATED TO VALERIE, ZOBIANA,
AND ALL THOSE WHO HAVE FOUGHT FOR FREEDOM OF UKRAINE
OR THE FREEDOM OF THE CREATURES OF WIND, WATER, AND EARTH

With thanks to the Ukrainian government for their gracious support, especially Ambassador of Ukraine to the USA Dr. Oleh Shamshur and Viktor Voloshyn, Cultural Attaché

Translations made Possible by the generous help of Andrij Kytasty, Kobzar

FORWARD BY ANDRIJ KYTASTY, KOBZAR

It has been said that history is written by the victors. So it is with the history of Ukraine, where Russian and Polish historians have conceived a history that has obscured and often maligned the Ukrainian Zaporozhian Kozaks. Perhaps with the recent downfall of the Soviet Union and the re-emergence of Ukraine as a sovereign nation in 1991, will a correct history become available to western scholars and Kozak enthusiasts.

The concept of the Kozak brotherhood, as evinced by historical reenactment and described in this handbook, captures much of the spirit that held the Kozaks to be uniquely called free men at a time when vast empires and fanatic religions battled for dominion.

Freed from tyranny by establishing a democratic rule of law, and defended bloodily by unequalled musket and sabre skills, the Kozaks established their reputation in the whole of Europe, especially as specialists in fighting the Turks.

Democratic rule of law allowed the Kozaks to elect the most able leader in time of war. This allowed the development and implementation of strategy and tactics far ahead of its time. Contrary to myth, the Zaporozhian Kozak was not cavalry, but best described as armored infantry. In defensive battle, they would circle their heavy wagons and be protected within while delivering withering unprecedented musket rate-of-fire upon an enemy. The most skilled rifleman would stand at the fore-front, fire a weapon and deliver it back, whereupon a loaded musket was passed to him from three or four re-loaders that stood to his rear. The Kozaks were also the first to implement amphibious warfare by choosing aquatic terrain to their advantage and as a force multiplier. They demonstrated legendary seamanship and sheer audacity in naval engagements and attacks against Turkish coastal fortification using their swift low-slung, unsinkable *chaikas*[1] on the Black Sea.

So powerful was the statement of a democracy in Europe in that time period, that one of the documents used by Thomas Jefferson in composing the Constitution of the United States of America was the Kozak constitution written by Hetman Pylyp Orlyk. The only true glimpse into the Kozak historical past with invaluable insights into their psychological and moral state of mind is offered in songs and *dumas*[2] of that time period that have been preserved to this day. This oral literature has been passed

---

[1] *Chaika* in Ukrainian means sea-gull. Their ships were made unsinkable by attaching hollow marsh bundles to the gunnels along the ship's length.
[2] Historical ballads.

down generation to generation by *Kobzari* [3] despite being persecuted and executed by every occupying regime.

Ukrainian history has been rewritten and the entire nation has been submerged for centuries. A genocide of 10 million souls was successfully executed in 1933 in the process of the final Russification and collectivization of Ukraine in Stalin's USSR. This fact remains largely unknown and even denied to this day.

Yet the whole works of one of the world's greatest poets, Taras Shevchenko, hinges around one thing—the unheard of freedom, heroics, and tragic demise of the Zaporozhian Kozaks.

It is hoped that the efforts of Kozak re-enactors, as sparked by the author of this handbook, will encourage study of this remarkable period of human struggle in a land called Ukraine, and cause a demand for truth to surface and ring out in clear song "…what they died for, why Kozak glory is known throughout the world…"[4]

Andrij the Kobzar with Author

---

[3] Bards, singers of dumas and historical songs.
[4] From Taras Shevchenko, Kobzar.

Козаку

This booklet has been written to provide a window into the life of mid-seventeenth century Ukraine, in particular that most misunderstood of characters…

The Knightly Brotherhood of the Zaporozhtsi!

The Kozaky reenactment group's goals, and hence those of this book:

I. To develop an authentic recreation of Kozaky (Cossacks) under Bohdan Khmelnitsky 1648 to 1657 with the typical camp followers.

II. To develop authentic (yet safe) recreations of dueling and military practices of the period.

III. To enjoy feasting, games, fellowship and lifestyle of the period.

IV. To promote the music and bardic (Kobzar) traditions of the Kozaky.

Statement of intent. Whilst recreating a period of intense racial, religious, sexual and social bigotry, every Kozaky re-enactor will respect and honor the diversity of the world in their 21st century lives and act in a socially acceptable manner.

"No religious quarrels amongst ourselves. He who breaks that rule is a deadman. Let one man escape that rule and we will all be dead by sundown." The Kapitain, The Last Valley…

Primary Contact Information

E-Mail - maks_zobi@msn.com
Web Group - http://groups.yahoo.com/group/kozakwars
Web Site - www-livinghistory.com

Suggested Basic Equipment and Authenticity Requirements

An excellent representation of both a male and female Kozak Artist: Victor Macklok

Re-enactors setting out to develop an individual character or found a new group will find it useful to set not only minimums of authenticity but a time line by which to meet those standards. Members should by their first anniversary reach the basic level of authentic kit as follows: basic footwear, Sharaváry (or skirts), sash, basic shirt (or blouse), and hat. If they are military personnel, then also: a **saber**, dagger, **long firearm**, **and powder container(s). Drinking vessel, bowl, spoon, and eating knife.** A member of the group's authenticity and safety counsel must approve all equipment.

1. **General:** No materials other than those available in the mid-seventeenth century shall be used. Specifically, no plastic, vinyl, aluminum, manmade fabrics, or other faux materials. The ***only*** exception to this is the use of ***environmentally unacceptable materials*** that may be replaced by very good quality replicas and passed by the group's Authenticity ***and*** Safety Councils.

2. **Sabers and Daggers:** Only those weapons that can be provenanced to the period 1600 to 1657 are acceptable. They must be blunted to a minimum of ***1/16th of an inch*** with a rounded point. All cutting edges will be free of sharp nicks and burrs. Whilst patina and natural bluing are acceptable on the blade, rust is not. All sword accoutrements such as baldrics and belts must be of period materials **and fit the rank and social standing of the character.** Both the Authenticity and Safety Councils must accept ***all*** blades (ask ***before*** you buy!). The maximum length of a dagger blade is 17". **Only daggers with hand guards may be used in dagger to dagger fighting, unless mail gloves are used. Gauntlets must be worn in all forms of fighting.**

3. **Armor and Helmets:** These must be provenanced to the period 1600 to 1657 and fit the rank and class of the character. In general, only ***very*** limited use by officers of high rank.

4. **Fire Arms:** Only those weapons that can be provenanced to the period 1600 to 1657 are acceptable. These must be in keeping with the rank and social position of the character. As a rule, long firearms are for Molodtsý, Churn, etc and pistols are for Onsauls and above.

5. **Men's Footwear:** Plain (no decorative stitching) brown or black **leather** boots or sandals (Postolý) of the period 1600 to 1657 may be worn. These must be in keeping with the rank and social position of the character. Red or Yellow may be used for Onsauls and above.

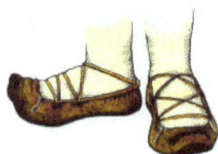

Postoly, these are an excellent low cost, yet very authentic option

6. **Men's Shirts:** *Only white/off white shirts* of the period 1600 to 1657 may be worn. These must be in keeping with the rank and social position of the character. Buttons, *if* used (rare in our period), must be wood, metal, bone (two hole only) or of the cloth dumpling type. The material should be linen; however, period looking mixes are acceptable. Care should be taken with embroidery. Ensure that there is only the correct amount/size and type for your character's rank and position; *none is far better*.

7. **Men's Trousers:** Sharaváry of the period 1600 to 1657 *or less baggy* trousers. Only natural pale browns and beiges for Moloytzy, red, black or other expensive dye colors for Onsúls and above (some may wish to cover better materials with tar). Materials for the garment and all decoration must be in keeping with the period.

8. **Men's Zhupán and Kontuse Coats:** Grey zhupán were most common, but any color or style of the period 1600 to 1657 may be worn. These must be in keeping with the rank and social position of the character. Buttons, must be wood, metal, or of the cloth dumpling type. Materials for the garment must be in keeping with the period (see typical Kozak full gear with black **Zhupán** right). Note typical horse hide "box" for accessories.

9. **Sash:** All members must wear a sash, normally darker colors for Moloytzy, red or **poyo** for Onsaúls and above. Higher ranks may have fancy silk types.

One correct Kozaky way to tie the sash

6

10.Men's Jewelry: A single hoop or simple pattern earring is normal, if worn it must be of the period and fit the standard criteria. Note: **eyeglasses** (considered Jewelry at the time), these must be period style, i.e. round horn or bone rim **without side bars**. *Eyeglasses were rare and very costly!*

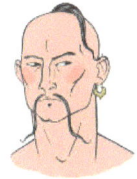

11.Hats: Must be should be worn by all Kozaky re-enactors unless they have a correct period hairstyle (as below) when in the public's view.

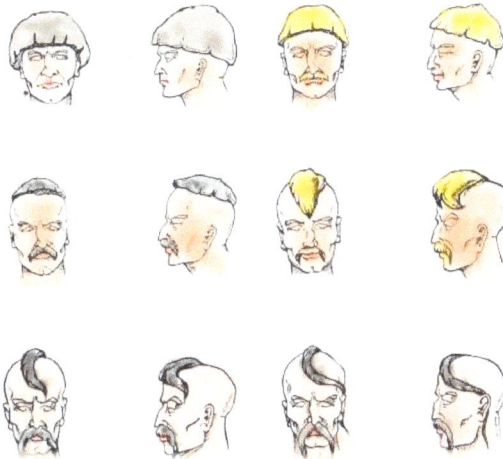

12.Women's Dress: Must fit the standard criteria for period, material, rank and class. A simple long skirt, white underskirt, apron, sash, white blouse, head covering, and shoes/boots make up a classic and authentic female attire. Remember vegetable dye colors only.

Women's clothing of the period by an unknown 19th century artist

13. Language: The use of a period mix of Ukrainian/Polish, Low German/Rotwelch, early modern English, and the language of your characters birth is requested. Please remember that children may be in the audience so care should be taken.

7

PERSONAL HISTORY

As part of the Kozaky organization's goal, it is important that **each member** attempt to research our period and their own families' history during this time. It is strongly suggested that, if possible, each member portray an ancestor, either historical or hypothetical. This character will provide a stimulus to authentic reenactment, especially in discussions with the general public and as basis/focus for research. The character should fit the general, ethnic and social background, rank, **gender**, etc. required by your group and the organization as whole. Each group's Authenticity Council will make all final decisions in this regard.

A special note in regard to gender: it is suggested that a maximum of one in twenty persons may represent a person trying to pass themselves off as the opposite sex. Whilst this was known at this time, it was not at all common, especially in Kozaky circles!

The Kozaky were made up of a wide range of European peoples, obviously Eastern Europeans will be more common, but it is known that there were German, French, Irish, Tartar, English, and even Turks in the ranks.

A SUGGESTED RANK SYSTEM

Rank: All members should join as ouchar, unless non-military, thereupon they join the tabor/baggage train at their appropriate social rank. In time, certain members **may** be promoted. Note: there should be no right to promotion just because a member has been with a group for a period of time. Promotion should be earned, in order to be considered for promotion the member may have shown exceptional progress in some of the following areas:

> **I, Authenticity of personal attire, arms, language, and equipment.**

> **II, Period skills such as sword work, building, arms manufacture, etc.**

> **III, Advancement of the group, either through enlistment, _funding_ of the group, building of equipment and/or structures, or through the development and dispersal of approved information.**

The conduct of any one person can negate any and all positive work done by a group or even a national organization. Remember, that we must be seen as members of a living history group, actors, historians, and not as street fighters or brawlers. The success and the very survival of the individual groups and the Kozaky revival depends on *our perceived* image.

A Kozak Rank System

Hetman	The Kozaky and Ukrainian Political/Military Chief	75
Koshovýj	Chief Otamán	40
Otamán	Colonel - Vatazhók, Banita, Kúreen Otamán	30
	The officers above are Nachalstrovo	
Sótnyk	Kapitain	25
Oboznyi	Quartermaster	20
Osaul	Aide-de-camp to the colonel	15
Khorunzhyi	Flag-bearer	
Bunchuzhnyi	Bunchuk bearer	
Pysar	Chancellor also known as a scribe	
Suddia	Judge/scribe	
Ensaul	Lower Officer	
Chern	Rank and file, but proven Kozaky - May wear red trousers	
Moloytzy	Unproven Kozaky	
Ouchar	New arrival	
Hotatá	Peasants	
Mudra Zhiulea	Wise Woman (held in high regard)	

The maximum rank any member may be dependent on the above conditions ***and the number of persons under their command.*** The suggested minimum number of persons under command for each rank is given in red on the right. The rank of otamán or its equal may be taken by founding members of any group. Special otamán terms include Vatazhók, denoting an unruly (even for those times) otamán; Banita is a highborn noble, turned outlaw, hounded by the courts so that he has escaped to the wild lands.

As rank played a limited role in the Kozaky lifestyle the only rules for addressing a higher officer is that they should be referred to as bat'ko or if in deference, bohatýr. Hats must be removed (and heads slightly bowed) only if the leading officer is making a speech or pronouncing judgment.

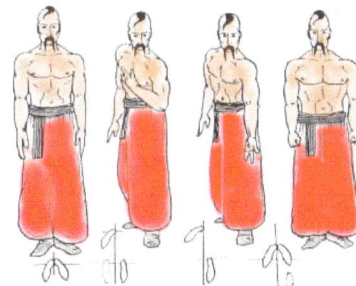

The correct Kozaky bow

The removing of the hat and the sweeping very low Kozaky bow is reserved for grand ladies, times you wish a lady to feel grand, and those of great rank on important occasions.

All Kozaky are known by their first name only unless formally referring to someone, then you would use their full name and rank. Many Kozaky had fanciful and descriptive names based on unusual or great moments in their lives or physical traits. These should be developed and used by any proven Kozak, making a good starting point for discussion s with the public.

The Kozak Oath

To join the ranks of the Kozaky, there were no questions asked regarding past rank, deeds or misdeeds, or even country of origin, only:

Do you hold Holy the Moist Mother Earth?
Do you hold Holy the Father?
Do you hold Holy the rising Son?

If the hotatá nodded in assent, a piece of earth was placed on their head and they were welcomed in to the knightly brotherhood of Kozaky and told to go to the Kurin of their choice. **Please note:** this is just one reconstructed version of the oath; some even asked if you drank horilka as an entry question!

The Rules of Live Blade Saber/Sword Play

Safety is the first concern of every member: safety for the general public, other members, and for each individual. Always regard the safety of the general public as the number one priority. They do not understand the inherent dangers of reenactment as we do. Help them; show them, teach them, but most of all, protect them.

Safety – Sword Work: All swordplay shall be conducted with safety as the first priority. All blades shall be of true high quality steel. They must be blunted to a minimum of $1/16^{th}$ of an inch with a rounded/flattened point. All cutting edges will be free of sharp nicks and burrs. Whilst patina and natural bluing are acceptable on the blade, rust is not. No sabre may weigh more than 3 lbs, less is always better. *The group's Authenticity and Safety Councils must accept all blades.*

All blades must be confirmed safe (blunted and free of nicks and burrs) by the safety officer or the ranking officer prior to every engagement.

All persons must be fully conversant with the concept of
BLOOD

B - Balance is the key to good control. Keep you legs bent, with your secondary weapon foot forward, where applicable.

L - Line is the understanding the direction and flow of combat. You must always be directly opposite your opponent and your bodyline in keeping with your action.

OO - Eye contact is essential to understand the intent of your opponent. You must watch your opponent at all times, not your weapon or their weapon.

D – Distance is vital to make safe blows. The safe distance must be kept always. Normally, this is just within a sword length's reach of your opponent. A good measure tends to be: if both opponents stand en garde, their blades should cross about 2-4 inches. Never close too rapidly or deeply on your opponent and never more than ***three*** fencing steps in any one attack.

I, **Areas of Strike**:

No blows above the top of the shoulder line.

No blows to the groin, this being above the knee on the inside of the leg to the hip line.

No full blows to the back center line.

In **dagger to dagger** fighting, **no** blows may be struck below the waist.

All of the above foul hits are counted as a kill to the one who made the foul attack.

Blows are acceptable to all limbs on the outside surface only, the inner arm being acceptable when the arm is extended. Blows to the arm must be above four fingers width from the wrist.

II, **Blows**:

All blows must be made with the **FLAT** of the blade, they should be made hard enough to feel, but ***no more.*** When using a saber the flat the blade should be used whenever possible, but light edge blows are acceptable. The wearing of ***hidden*** modern athletic cups, knee pads, etc. is recommended.

The idea is to score a point, NOT to harm your opponent!

III, Cuts:

Made with the flat of the blade. If using a rapier, cuts **must be drawn** or they will merely be a scratch and not count. Swords and sabers need only make contact. **Remember, they should be made hard enough to feel but, no more!**

In **dagger to dagger** fighting, blows should be in the form of a *light* punching action, the blade must be completely flat against the body, and no drawing of the blade is necessary. Chain mail gauntlets must me used in dagger fighting unless a full hand guard is mounted on the dagger.

A correctly struck cut with a rapier shall render that limb useless. The weapon of choice must be dropped immediately. If the CUT was to a leg, the weapon of that side must be dropped and the leg grasped momentarily before resuming combat. Any further hit to that leg counts as a KILL (from blood loss). With a CUT to the arm, that weapon is dropped immediately. Any further hit to a limb counts as a KILL (from blood loss). These CUTS count as a hit in practice and other scoring events, and is 10 points. **If using a saber, all legal blows count as a KILL.**

A correctly struck cut to the trunk of the body shall count as a KILL. The killed person must then drop his weapons safely and die in suitable agony over a reasonable time. *No further blows may be made by a dying person.* This is counted as a KILL in practice and other scoring events, and is 20 points. If the KILL is the first hit, then 25 points are scored.

A cut may also be counted by **gently tapping** the weapon to the opponents back. This is a KILL (20 or 25 points). NEVER strike an opponent when down this is a foul shot.

IV, Thrusts:

These may only be made by those persons who have suitable experience and temperament. **This decision shall be made by the Safety Council after a formal test and examination**.

No thrusts may be made with a dagger or saber.

"Thrusts" may be executed with a <u>rapier</u> in *only* one of two manners:
A, The broken wrist hit. As the blade *NEARS* the body, the wrist (held in pronation only) is dropped rapidly down and back. The hit is made either by the flat of the blade only. The hit must not be heavy. This is the safest and preferred method of thrust.

B. A Touch. A literal light touch with the tip of the blade**.** *No impact must be made*. This must be done only when you are certain of full control and should be done in conjunction with a broken wrist movement.

For duels and other scoring events: If a kill is made before a hit has been made to either party a **CLEAN KILL** has been made and counts as 25 points.

V. Firearms: All firearms must be approved by the Safety Council. **No firearm brought onto the field may be able to discharge a projectile at <u>full</u> and <u>lethal</u> velocity.**

Drilled barrels, oversize/multiple touchholes, and blow back releases are preferred. However minimal charges *may* be acceptable to the group's Safety Council. A minimum of 30' feet shall be used between units when using firearms. Before issuing the order to fire, the ranking officer must visually confirm that all ramrods have been removed. He will then call KLAR! The firing may then and only then commence. For public events **kills from shots fired shall be drawn by lots before the battle,** except those deemed vital (by both sides) to the plot of the scenario.

VI. Pikes, Half Pikes, Spears, Farm Implements, and Horse Axes : Should only be used in an upright position for the "push of pike" in battle. Horse axes, etc. may be used in duels and single combat with the weapon's head counting the same as a rapier cut. ONLY pre-arranged duels may be fought in a battle situation if both the safety and historical officers agree.

VII. **In Regard to Armors**. Leather acts as armor to rapier, dagger, and horse axe only. A saber will cut through any non steel armor.

VIII. All duels counting towards the half or full year awards must be judged by a third person. This judge has final say, unless the person receiving the blow states it was fair and the judge felt not, only then may a judge be overridden. In competitions, three judges should be used, with the highest ranked judge acting as head judge in disputes. No one may challenge a decision made by the three judges.

SPECIAL RULE: No drinking of alcoholic beverages, heavy medications, or the use of strong herbs on the day of a duel or battle *until after the event and all weapons have been removed.* The severest of punishments should be reserved for *ANYONE* breaking this rule!

Kozaky
Artist: A. Bazylevych

A Historical Note for the Khmelnit'sky Period Kozak:

For the first part of the rebellion almost all Kozaky were **not** mounted. Most Kozaky fought as they always had, as infantry. Even those Kozaky with mounts, normally dismounted and fought as dragoons did, unless they had previous experience of mounted warfare, such as serving with Polish registered regiments or nobles.

Many fought with simple farm tools at first, picking up better weapons as they gained victories. Some peasants retained simple fighting equipment as a symbol of their rebellious status. The whirlwind of the rebellion caught up many different ethnic groups, Poles, Germans, etc. It was a very prudent course of action to go with the flow with the rebellion's tide rather fight overwhelming odds and a gruesome death at the hands of the angry mob. Some persona may wish to represent these poor folks, giving them an option to change sides at the first opportunity, or not!

Period graffiti of armed peasants

A Kozaky Glossary A (must be known)

	Orders	
Vperéd	**Advance**	**Ukr.**
Na Livo	**To the Left**	**Ukr.**
Na Pravo	**To the Right**	**Ukr.**
Stani	**Halt**	**Ukr.**
Nazad	**Go Back**	**Ukr.**
Spasajtesia	**Run for Your Life!**	**Ukr.**
	Shouts	
Volia	**Freedom!**	**Ukr.**
V bij braty	**To war my brothers!**	**Ukr.**
Na Slavu!	**To glory!**	**Ukr.**
Puhu Puhu	**Hello, literally Eagle Owl (to) Eagle Owl**	**Ukr.**

A KOZAKY GLOSSARY B (Best known - Red first)

Baba	Old woman (may be derogatory)	Ukr
Heŕoj	Hero (more recent)	Ukr
Banchuk	Hetman/Otaman's horse tail standard	Pol/Ukr
Banita	High-born outlaw Kozaky leader (Maks, for example)	Ukr
Bat'ko	Father/sir/Uncle	Ukr
Biz Zabiz	Hussaria war chant	Pol
Bohaťyr	Warrior Hero	Ukr.
Bulawá	Hetman's mace	Pol/Ukr
Cháika	Kozak long boat	Ukr
Chern	Rank and file Kozak	Ukr
Chremiss	Ancient race of wild hunters	Ukr
Chuvash	Ancient race of wild hunters Look like Finns, worship Wooden Statue of "St. Nicholas".	Ukr
Dývo	A wonder/magic	Ukr
Dúrnen	Dumb head	Ukr
Onsúl	Lower officer	Ukr.
Gojhalka/Samolón	Home made vodka	Ukr.
hototá	Homeless lower peasants	Ukr
Spasý Hóspody	Gott save us!	Ukr.
Hosudár	Lord King	Ukr
Hetman	Commander in chief	Pol/Ukr.
Hóspody Pomýlooj	Gott have mercy	Ukr
Hulay Horodyny	Siege tower (with canon)	Ukr
khútir	Farmstead	Ukr
Kniahýna	Princess	Ukr
Kniaz	Prince	Ukr
Kokoshynk	Beaded Kozak woman's headdress	Ukr
Mudra Zhiulna	Wise woman	Ukr
Koncerze	Tuck	Pol
Kórtchuma	Tavern	Ukr.
Koshovyj	Chief Otaman	Ukr
Krivonos	Crooked nose	Ukr.

Kúreen	Kozak Encampment	Ukr
Kunack	A brother of the Kozaky	Ukr
Liakh	Pole (derogatory)	Ukr
Lýtzari	Knights /Hussaria	Ukr
Máty	Mother	Ukr
Maydàn	Open field	Tartar/ Ukr
Mirhorodsty	Kozak from Mirhorod	Ukr
Molodytsý	Young Kozaky	Ukr
Mordvas	Ancient race of wild hunters of the forests with red hair. Women wear short black skirts, with white bandaged legs.	Ukr
Na sh'chastye	For good luck	Ukr
Na Slavu	For glory!	Ukr
Na umor	To the death (drink)	Ukr
Na Zdorovye	For health	Ukr
Nachalstro	Higher Officers	Ukl
Ne právda	Not true	Ukr
Ne Strilàt	(no) fire	Ukr
Osoledets	Kozak Scalplock (herring cut)	Ukr
Otamán	Kozak leader	Ukr.
Ouchar	Young Kozak (without battle experience)	Ukr
Pa'neh	Sir, lord, master	Ukr
Polk	Regiment	Ukr
Polkóvnyk	Master of a "battle" or Kozak company	Ukr
Piernacz	Smaller Otaman's mace	Ukr
Pistoléty	Pistol	Pol
Postolý	Moccasin like shoe	Ukr
Pynernatch	Short bone & cherry wood baton for safe conduct	Ukr
Ráda	Kozak meeting/council	Ukr
Sharaváry	Wide pleated trousers Note: Off white or other brighter (natural) colors. Higher ranks wore red silk often covered in tar. Green only worn by the foolhardy due to Moslem Hajjis.	Ukr
Shtcho s'tobyu	What's wrong with you?	Ukr
Sietch	The Kozak Stronghold	Ukr
Sietchovtsy	Kozaky of the Seitch	Ukr
Slava bóhu	God be praised (greeting)	Ukr
Sotnia	"Hundred" Kozak Company or "battle"	Ukr

Sótnyk	Master of "Hundred" Kozak Company or "battle"	Ukr
Spasájsia	Mercy/Save yourselves!	Ukr
Starosta	Sheriff	Ukr
Starostvo	County	Pol/ Ukr
Steej	Halt	Ukr.
Shàblia	Sabre	Ukr
Shliákhta	Nobility	Ukr
Ta' nicholo	It Doesn't matter	Ukr.
Tabor	Armed wagon train/camp	Ukr
Tchaban	Horse herder	Ukr
Tchambul	Tatar cohort	Tartar/ Ukr
Vataha	Kozak cohort	Ukr
Vatazlók	Kozak Leader	Ukr
Viéche	Ancient full council	Ukr
Voyevóde	Palatine/state ruler	Ukr
Yarmarok	Harvest faire (wild)	Ukr
Yassýr	Slave/slavery	Tartar/ Ukr
Zabýtýj	Dead	Ukr
Zaporózhtzi	Kozaky of Zaporohje	Ukr
Zaporohje	Lower Dnieper	Ukr
Zdron	Stay healthy - sound of a horse's snort	Pol/Ukr
Zhupán	Long Coat (under coat)	Ukr

Kozaky Toasts

A horse has four legs, A Kozak has four things;
Meat, Vodka, good boots, and St. Nick to watch over me!

To the faith, to all the knightly brother
Kozaky wherever they may be in the world!

He who raises a cup of vodka to me, A friend
He who raises a cup of vodka to me, and drains it to the dregs in one,
A friend and sworn brother!

Kozak
Artist: A. Bazylevych

How to make a pair of Sharavary

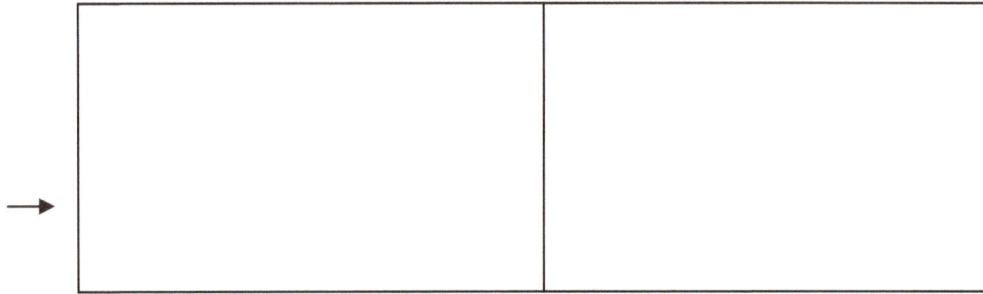

Take one length of cloth, only natural pale browns and beige wool or linen for Moloytzy, red, blue, yellow, etc. for Ensauls and above (some may wish to cover better materials with tar). Materials must be in keeping with the period and rank.

Depth/height must be enough for distance from waist to **ankle or more.**
Fold in half and sew side seam at arrow, this seam goes to the front center line

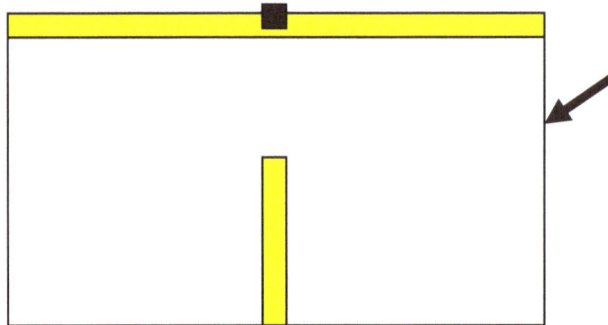

Cut up the center (vertical shaded area) to form legs,
ensuring enough depth for crotch
Sew well along new seam area (vertical shaded area)
Fold over top to allow easy passage of chosen cord sew seam
(top horizontal shaded area) leave small gap in this roll at the front to
allow cord to be tied in front (dark shaded area). Sides may be cut at an
angle narrowing at the waist from the base at the bottom of the Sharaváry.
Gather material along cord (and ankle if wished) and that is it!

Materials required
3-6 yards of 44"-48" cloth
(these trousers can be moderately tight fitting to baggy)
Cord
Needle and thread

How to make a Kozak Shirt

Take a double sized *linen* sheet or any linen cloth wide enough to reach as far as you want the sleeves. It is period to have shorter sleeves. Fold so that the fold is at your shoulder. (Silk may be used by high officers)

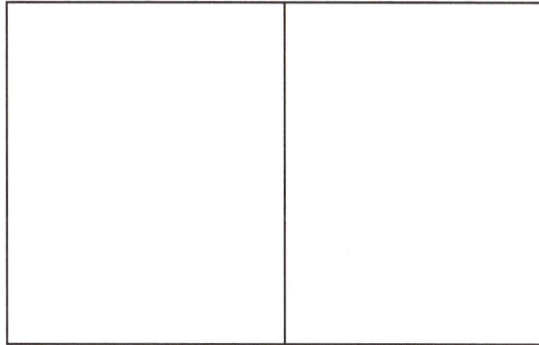

Cut in the shape below, to *loosely* fit your size.

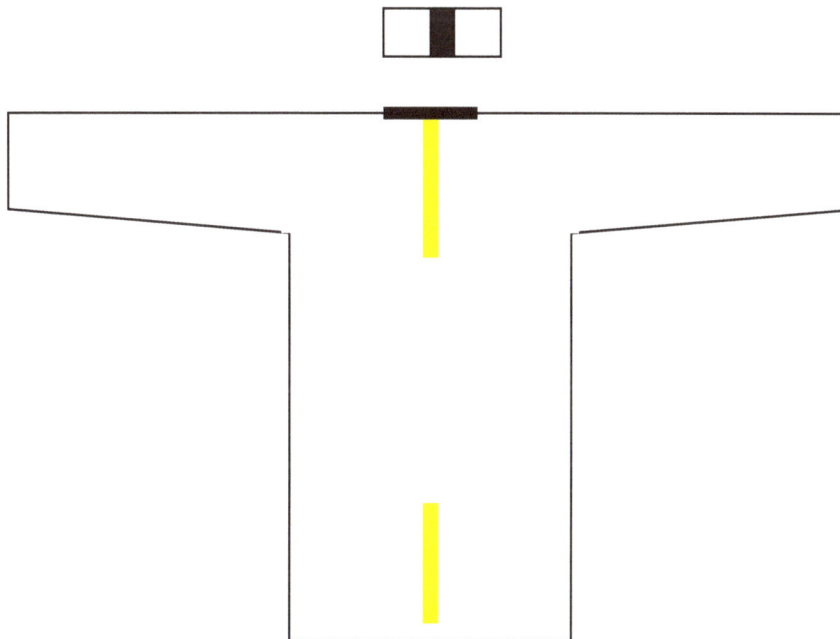

Sew side seams well. Slit where the yellow is marked, roll and sew seams.
Add collar and tie closure if wished.
Please note: this is a period construction. The correct constructional method is available from several resources, this a period looking garment for your first development of your character.

A Kozaky Song

(With certain alterations due to the highly racial nature of original)

Grief has fallen on our mother country, she has nowhere to go,
The horses of the horde have trampled our little ones,
The little ones they trampled, the old they cut down,
The young and fair took to slavery.

> *Oh I was serving, I served a Polish lord,*
> *Now I will serve him no more,*
> *Oh I was serving, I served a Moslem lord*
> *But now I will be serving our own Hetman!*

Wake up glorious Mother-Country, Brothers to the Ukraine,
Cut down altogether the leaseholders, mix their blood with our yellow sand,
Do not let your faith be dishonored,
Give not way to the foreign day,

> *Oh I was serving, I served a Polish lord,*
> *Now I will serve him no more,*
> *Oh I was serving, I served a Turkish lord*
> *But now I will be serving our own Hetman!*

Rise up the bold young men, to the Brotherhood
To chase away the lord and his leaseholder from our Mother,
Any who did not have even a torn sheepskin coat,
Can now put on the rich crimson clothes!

> *Oh I was serving, I served a Polish lord,*
> *Now I will serve him no more,*
> *Oh I was serving, I served a Turkish lord*
> *But now I will be serving our own Hetman!*

I call to you, oh you lords and leaseholders,
When the quiet wind from Kozaky land blows
Your whole grand guard shall flee
To run away from Khmelnytsky our Hetman!

> *Oh I was serving, I served a Polish lord,*
> *Now I will serve him no more,*
> *Oh I was serving, I served a Turkish lord*
> *But now I will be serving our own Hetman!*

Come all the bold young men to the Brotherhood,
And you Srul, take matchlock, powder, and lead
And you Czui take the ramrod to cannon
And you Janush take sabre bright to open their necks

Oh I was serving, I served a Polish lord,
Now I will serve him no more,
Oh I was serving, I served a Turkish lord
But now I will be serving our own Hetman!

Unknown 19th Century Artist

The Following historical notes are given only as an early rough guide to assist you, the re-enactor in developing an accurate mid seventeenth century Kozaky persona/character. These notes have been extensively researched and verified. However, they are a personal view of the author and should not be taken as the only view of these events, persons, times and events.

You are strongly recommended to carry out your own research and form your own views.

ЗАПОRЗНIA

The Zaporizhia, is a name of both the military and political organization of the Kozaky and their territory in Southern Ukraine from the mid-16th century to 1775. The name was derived from the territory's location "beyond the rapids" (Zaporohamy). Its center was the Zaporozhian Sich. The Zaporizhia's territory the was considered to be situated to the south and east of Polish-ruled Right-Bank Ukraine, from which it was separated by the Boh River, and the Tiasmyn River, a tributary of the Dnieper River.

The Kozaky had gained renown in the late 15th century as defenders of the Lithuanian-Ruthenian state against the Crimean Tatars, while serving the Cherkasy and Kaniv starostas and living as free brigands in the un-colonized wild steppe frontier of the Polish Lithuanian state. The rise of the Zaporizhia resulted from the increasing colonization of that frontier by Ukrainians, Germans, Austrians and even French fleeing serfdom and other oppressions, these horrors became even worse during the Thirty Years War (1618-48). However, many Kozaky served in the Thirty Years War on all sides, generally known as Croats at the time. The Kozaky established homesteads and, to defend themselves from Tatar raids, built fortified camps (sichi), which were later united to create a central fortress, the Zaporozhian Sich, under the leadership of Dmytro Vyshnevetsky on Mala Khortytsia Island (ca

1552). The anti-Noble/Polish Kozak rebellions of the 1590s, 1620s, and 1630s originated in the Zaporizhia and resulted in the growth of the military and political strength of the Zaporozhian host. The Zaporizhia played a very key role in the period of the Kozak-Polish War of 1648 to 57. During the following period, often named the times of Ruin, it influenced the course of events negatively. Less politically sophisticated Zaporozhian leaders were exploited by Muscovy, Ottoman Turkey, and the Crimean Khanate, they often succeeded in pitting the Zaporizhia against their natural ally, the Hetman state.

Portrait of an old Kozak - Artist unknown

The Zaporizhia became an ally of Hetman Ivan Mazepa and thus Charles XII of Sweden in 1709. In retaliation, Russian forces destroyed the Chortomlyk Sich, and after their victory at the Battle of Poltava, mercilessly exterminated the Zaporozhians. Their fate after this period is not (thankfully) within our period of reenactment and is a sad story.

A unique sociopolitical order evolved in the Zaporizhia; and with certain small changes, it existed until the end of the 18th century. The order was based on the political and social equality of all Zaporozhian Kozaky regardless of their social/ethnic origins. The principle of general elections was applied to all representative bodies, including the Supreme Sich Council, the central administrative body, known as the Kosh of the Zaporozhian Sich, the Kosh otaman and his starshyna (the Kosh judge, chancellor, onsaul, and quartermaster), and the Otamans of the Zaporozhian kurins (Kosh is from the Turkic Kos – Group of yurts, stable stall, or troop). Those elected figures constituted the Council of Officers, the administrative body. Later, outside the Sich appointed colonels commanded several districts called palankas. The Kozak elective meeting/body was known as a Rada. When this was a full election it was sometimes called the Chorna Rada or Black Council.

At the Sich, the Zaporozhian host (army) was traditionally divided into 38 Kurins; each Kurin had several hundred Kozaky. The number of Kurins was actually higher, because several existed outside the Sich. Each Kurin was further divided into companies of 100 men, the sotnia. Later, numerous Zymivnyk, or homesteads, on the territory of each palanka were inhabited by married Kozaky, since only unmarried Kozaky could live for long periods at the Sich.

A period representation of a Rada at the Sich

Collective farming was undertaken by each kurin. Fishing, hunting, and raising cattle were the chief occupations in the Zaporozhian. The Zaporizhia also played an important commercial role because of its location on the trade route from the Crimea to Poland, Moscovy, and later, the Hetman state

A seal of the *Zaporozhian* host

Ukrainian-Polish War 1648-57

The Ukrainian-Polish War also known as the Kozak rebellion or Ukrainian War of Independence, depending on whose side you're on, began in 1648. It seemed like the typical Kozak uprising but quickly turned into a war of the Ukrainian populace, particularly the Kozaky and peasants, against the Polish Commonwealth. Hetman Bohdan Khmelnytsky assumed leadership of the Ukrainian forces. The war has generally been divided into these several phases.

January to November 1648. In this period, a series of brilliant Kozak victories aroused the people and won wide support for Bohdan Khmelnytsky. What was strictly a Kozaky rebellion became transformed into a mass movement against the Polish magnate's power…

On 21 January 1648, Khmelnytsky led a small unit of registered Kozaky and Zaporozhian Kozaky in an attack on the Polish garrison on Bazavluk Lake, on the Dnieper River, and overpowered it. This freed the Zaporozhian Sich from Polish control and won the Zaporozhian Kozaky over to Khmelnytsky's side. He was elected hetman. The subsequent months were spent in preparations for a larger rebellion. Proclamations were sent out urging the Kozaky, peasants, and burghers to rise against the nobility. Khmelnytsky concluded an *apparently* important treaty with Turkey and the Crimean khan Islam-Girei III, obtaining the aid of a 40,000-strong Tatar army under Tuhai-Bei's leadership.

The Polish government sent an army of 30,000 men in April 1648 to suppress the uprising in Ukraine. The Polish commanders expected little opposition and made a serious tactical blunder by dividing their forces. About 10,000 rebels surrounded the Polish advance guard of 5,000 men, led by Stephan Potocki, Hetman Miklo Potocki's son, at Zhovti Vody (Yellow Waters).This army was destroyed in a siege and retreat

Winged Hussar re-enactor, Rik Fox in battle

by 16 May 1648. Khmelnytsky and the Tatar army met the main Polish force, commanded by Grand Hetman Miklo Potocki and Field Hetman Marcin Kalinowski, near Korsun and routed it on 26 May 1648. The two Polish commanders were captured by the Tatars. After these victories, fighting between Kozak-peasant detachments and Polish troops flared up throughout Ukraine. In the summer of 1648, the detachment of Colonel Maksym Kryvonis (Crooked Nose) engaged in several bloody battles with the Polish nobility's force, led by Prince Jeremini Winiowiecki. During this fighting, the population suffered terrible depredations. The Polish troops systematically killed any suspected Kozaky sympathizers, peasants, including women, children, and the old people who fell into their hands, while the rebels treated the nobles, Catholic clergy and Jewish leaseholders, many of whom took the side of the Polish nobles, in a similar fashion.

At the end of the summer, the Polish government sent another well-equipped army of 32,000 Poles and 8,000 German mercenaries against the Kozaky. The army's command, consisting of A. Koniecpolski, M. Ostrora, and Prince Wadysaw-Dominik Zasawski, was weak and inexperienced.

Kozaky against Hussaria by the artist Dan Horsechief

Jeremini Wiowiecki, who wanted to be the commander in chief of the Polish forces, did not have adequate communications with the advancing Polish army. Confident of victory, the Polish commanders let Bohdan Khmelnytsky assume a very convenient position near Pyliavtsi. During the battle that took place there on 23 September 1648, the rebels, numbering about 80,000, completely crushed the Polish army. Khmelnytsky's army, now of about 100,000 men, marched into the Western Ukraine, and in early November, besieged Lviv. Several Kozak detachments advanced west into territories settled mostly by Poles or Belarusians, and anti-noble and anti-Polish revolts also broke out throughout Southern and Eastern Poland. At the request of the Ukrainian burghers, Khmelnytsky lifted the siege of Lviv and besieged Zamoaz, where the remnants of Wiowiecki's army had sought refuge. With the November election of a new Polish king, Jan II Casimir Vasa, whose candidacy was supported by Khmelnytsky, the Ukrainian army returned to the Dnieper region, and on 2 January 1649, triumphantly entered Kyiv.

April to August 1649. Bohdan Khmelnytsky decided to completely separate Ukraine from Poland, but although he continued to triumph on the battlefield, he could not overpower the Polish army. Mobilizing all the forces of the Polish Commonwealth, Jan II Casimir Vasa began the offensive against Khmelnytsky in April 1649. The main Polish force under the command of the king himself departed from Volhynia, while the Lithuanian army, commanded by the Lithuanian hetman, Prince J. Radziwill, marched on Kyiv. On 10 July, Khmelnytsky and Islam-Girei III surrounded a part of the king's forces in Zbarazh. When Jan II Casimir Vasa with his army of 25,000 men went to the aid of the besieged troops, Khmelnytsky led a surprise attack on 15 August and encircled the king at Zboriv. In the meantime, during June and July, the Lithuanian army almost reached Kyiv, but the constant Kozak raids and peasant partisan fighting in the rear forced the Lithuanians to retreat. A decisive and final victory over the Poles appeared to be within Khmelnytsky's grasp, but at this critical moment Islam-Girei III, who was bribed by the Poles and disturbed by the rapid growth of the Ukrainian forces, withdrew his troops, which forced Khmelnytsky to negotiate with the Poles. On 28 August 1649, Khmelnytsky concluded the Treaty of Zboriv with the Polish delegation headed by Jerzy Ossolinski. The treaty could not really satisfy either side, as the goals of the rebellion had changed and expanded greatly.

August 1650 to September 1651. International factors began to play a more important role in the Ukrainian-Polish conflict. The Kozaky experienced their first defeats and were forced to retreat from the positions they had won previously. In the summer of 1650, both sides tried to isolate each other by diplomatic means. Polish diplomats warned Moscow about the Kozak threat and succeeded in gaining the support of Vasile Lupu, the hospodar of Moldavia. Bohdan Khmelnytsky tried to strengthen his contacts with the Crimean Tatars and the Ottoman Porte. To undermine Polish influence in Moldavia, Khmelnytsky sent a large Kozak-Tatar army there in August 1650, and forced Vasile Lupu to sign a treaty and to promise to give his daughter Roksana Lupu in marriage to Khmelnytsky's son Tymish Khmelnytsky.

While the Kozaky were busy in Moldavia, a Polish army of 50,000 men attacked the Bratslav region on 20 February 1651. A major battle took place in June near the town of Berestechko in Volhynia. The Polish army, which included about 20,000 German states mercenaries who were all highly trained veterans of the Thirty Years War, faced the Ukrainian-Tatar forces. The Kozaky were betrayed ***once again*** by the Tatars and were defeated. On 10 July, they retreated under difficult conditions to Bila Tserkva. At the beginning of August, the Lithuanian army occupied and ravaged Kyiv. In spite of these setbacks, Bohdan Khmelnytsky mobilized a force of 50,000 men, and on 24 to 25 September 1651, engaged the enemy in battle near Bila Tserkva. The fighting was fierce but inconclusive. Drained of strength, both sides began negotiations, which led to a treaty unfavorable to Khmelnytsky. This is known as the "Treaty of Bila Tserkvaâ," and was signed on 28 September. Soon after the signing of the treaty, Polish troops and nobles began to return to Ukraine to restore the former order of serfdom to the peasants. Much of the population of Right-Bank Ukraine, threatened by the return of their former oppressors, began to abandon their villages and migrated east to Left-Bank Ukraine.

Spring 1652 to winter 1653. Although the Kozaky scored several victories against the Poles, signs of fatigue and discouragement appeared, and Bohdan Khmelnytsky began to rely increasingly on foreign help. In 1651, he, as it turned out, disastrously strengthened his ties with the Tatars and the Porte. He focused his attention on Moldavia, hoping that Tymish Khmelnytsky's marriage with Roksana Lupu would solidify the alliance of Ukraine with Moldavia and indirectly with Turkey and the Crimean Khanate. In the spring of 1652, Khmelnytsky sent Tymish with a large

Kozak-Tatar army to Moldavia. On 2 June, the army encountered a Polish force of 30,000 men at Batih, and Khmelnytsky, who had been forced to come to his son's aid, scored a brilliant victory. In August 1652, Tymish married Roksana, but in the spring of 1653, the Moldavian boyars, supported by Wallachia and Transylvania, revolted against Vasile Lupu and the Kozaky. Tymish died defending Suceava. His death on 15 September 1653 put an end to Khmelnytsky's Moldavian orientation. In the meantime, war again broke out in Ukraine. A large Polish army of 80,000 men invaded Podilia; however, they were encircled at Zhvanets by the combined forces of the Kozaky and Tatars at the beginning of December 1653. At a critical moment, the Tatars *once again* concluded an agreement with the Poles, forcing Bohdan Khmelnytsky to make peace with the Poles on 5 December on the basis of the conditions of the Treaty of Zboriv of 1649. This latest act of Tatar treachery finally convinced Khmelnytsky to change his foreign policy!

Bohdan Khmelnytsky had maintained diplomatic relations with Muscovy almost from the beginning of the rebellion, but Tsar Aleksei Mikhailovich refused to support the uprising, for this would lead to war with Poland. The Polish defeats and the danger of Khmelnytsky's acceptance of the Porte's suzerainty, however, persuaded Moscow to resume negotiations with the hetman in 1653. These negotiations culminated in the Pereiaslav Treaty of 1654, according to which Ukraine recognized the protectorate of the Russian tsar while supposedly maintaining it's complete autonomy and received Russian military and political aid against Poland.

Summer 1654 to autumn 1657. In this period, the united Ukrainian and Muscovite forces took the offensive against Poland and scored significant victories. Major battles took place in Right-Bank Ukraine, Belarus, and Western Ukraine. In the summer of 1654, the Muscovite army and 20,000 Kozaky, led by Ivan Zolotarenko, invaded Belarus and captured Smolensk. Continuing the campaign in 1657, they took Vilnius in July. During the Belarusian campaigns, a tension arose between the allies over the question of which side should control the captured
territories, the Zaporozhian Host or Moscow. In the meantime, the Poles invaded the Bratslav region in the fall of 1654, and on 20 January 1657, laid siege to Uman. Bohdan Khmelnytsky and the Russian commander, Vasilii Sheremetev, led a joint army of 70,000 men against the enemy and fought a hard but inconclusive battle near Okhmativ on 29 January 1657. In the spring, the Ukrainian-Muscovite forces invaded Western Ukraine, and by the end of September, they besieged Lviv. In October, however, when Poland's new allies, the Tatars, arrived with reinforcements, the Kozaky and Russians retreated east.

Autumn 1656 to summer 1657. Bohdan Khmelnytsky became increasingly disappointed with the Russians, and he began to look for other allies against Poland. In the summer of 1657, the Swedish king, Charles X Gustav, took advantage of Poland's war with the Kozaky and Russians to seize the northern part of Poland and Lithuania. Moscow became perturbed at the growth of Swedish power. Hence, on 24 October 1656, it signed the Vilnius Peace Treaty with Poland and then jointly with Poland declared war on Sweden. The Ukrainian government, whose representatives were excluded from the negotiations, was very indignant over the peace treaty. Hence, in October 1656, in spite of Russian protests, Bohdan Khmelnytsky entered into a broad coalition with Sweden, Transylvania, Brandenburg, Moldavia, and Wallachia. The coalition had as its purpose, the partition of Poland. In joining the coalition, the hetman was interested mainly in capturing the Western Ukrainian territories and uniting them with Ukraine. The interests of the coalition members diverged. Furthermore, Poland obtained diplomatic and military support from Austria, Muscovy, and the Crimea. In spite of this, a Ukrainian-Transylvanian army of 30,000 Hungarians and 20,000 Kozaky under the command of Colonel Antin Zhdanovych invaded Poland in January 1657, and occupied Galicia and a large part of Poland, including Cracow and Warsaw, but the oppression of the local population by the Hungarians and the intrigues hatched by Muscovite agents among the Kozaky diminished the army's fighting capacity. The Hungarians were forced to retreat eastward before the Polish offensive. Towards the end of July 1657, they were encircled by the Poles and Tatars at Medzhybizh and were forced to sign the Treaty of Chornyi Ostriv on 22 July. Zhdanovych tried to hold the anti-Polish front, but did not succeed. This catastrophe hastened the death of Khmelnytsky, which occurred on 6 August 1657. This marked the end of the Kozak-Polish War of Independence, but not the wars for the Ukraine.

The Hetman rides to victory
Artist: Victor Macklok

Bohdan Khmelnytsky

Bohdan Zinovii Khmelnytsky (Xmel'nyc'ky) was born in 1595 or 6, He died in August 1657 in Chyhyryn. He was Hetman of the Zaporozhian host from 1648 to 1657 and founder of the Hetman state (1648–1782). By birth, he belonged to the Ukrainian lesser nobility and bore the Massalski, and later the Abdank coat of arms. His father, Mykhailo Khmelnytsky, served as an officer under the Polish crown, Hetman Stanislaw Zolkiewski. His mother, according to most sources, was of Kozak descent. Khmelnytsky's place of birth has not been determined for certain. Little more is known about Khmelnytsky's education, but he received his elementary schooling in Ukrainian, and his secondary and higher education in Poland at a Jesuit college, possibly in Lviv. He completed his schooling before 1620; however, he acquired a broad knowledge of world history, fluency in Polish, Latin, Turkish, Tatar and French, and the art of diplomacy. The Battle of Cecora (1620), in which he lost his father and was captured by the Turks, was his first military action. After spending two years in Istanbul, he was ransomed by his mother and returned to the Polish Ukraine.

I could find no reliable information about Khmelnytsky's activities from 1622 to 1637. All later accounts of his exploits in wars against Tatars, Turks, and Russians (1632–4) have little documentary foundation. Only one fact is certain, in the 1620s, he joined the registered Kozaky. Sometime between 1625 and 1627, he married Hanna Somko, a Kozak's daughter from Pereiaslav, and settled on his patrimonial estate in Subotiv near Chyhyryn. By 1637, heattained the high office of military chancellor. His signature appears on the capitulation agreement signed at Borovytsia on 24 December 1637,

A period portrait of the Hetman
Unknown artist

which marked the end of a Kozak rebellion.

There is evidence to support the theory that Khmelnytsky belonged to the faction of officers who favored an understanding between the Zaporozhian Host and Poland. Subsequent events, however, dashed any hopes of reconciliation. By the Ordinance of 1638, the Polish king revoked the autonomy of the Zaporozhian Host and placed the registered Kozaky under the direct authority of the Polish military command in Ukraine. The Office of Military Chancellor, which Khmelnytsky had held, was abolished and Khmelnytsky was demoted to a captain of the Chyhyryn regiment. In the fall of 1638, he visited Warsaw with a Kozak delegation to petition King Wladyslaw IV Vasa to restore the former Kozak privileges. In the next few years,

Khmelnytsky devoted his attention mostly to his estates in the Chyhyryn region, but in 1645, he served with a detachment of 2,000–2,500 Kozaky in *France*, and probably took part in a siege at Dunkirk (one of many).

By this time, his reputation for leadership was such that King Wladyslaw IV Vasa, in putting together a coalition of The Holy Roman Empire, Poland, Venice, and other states against Turkey, turned to him to obtain the support of the Zaporozhian Kozaky. In April 1646, he was one of the Kozak envoys in Warsaw with whom the king discussed plans for the impending war. These events contributed to his reputation in Ukraine, Poland, and abroad, and provided him with wide military and political contacts. Khmelnytsky, however, had been regarded with suspicion for many years by the Polish magnates in Ukraine who were politically opposed to King Wladyslaw IV Vasa, possibly due to his evident interest in the Kozaky as a military force. The new landowners of the Chyhyryn region, A. Koniecpolski, Crown Hetman Stanislaw Zolkiewski, and his son, Crown Flag-bearer A. Zolkiewski, treated Khmelnytsky with particular hostility. With the collusion of the Chyhyryn, assistant vicegerent D. Czaplinski, who bore some personal grudge against Khmelnytsky, conspired to deprive Khmelnytsky of his Subotiv estate. In spite of the fact that Khmelnytsky received a royal title to Subotiv in 1646, Czaplinski raided the estate, seized movable property, and disrupted the manor's economy. At the same time, Czaplinski's servants beat Khmelnytsky's small son to death. Under these conditions of violence and terror, Khmelnytsky's wife died in 1647. Towards the end of that fateful year, Koniecpolski ordered Khmelnytsky's arrest and execution. It was only the help and the monies put up by his friends among the Chyhyryn officers, and particularly by Col Mykhailo Krychevsky, that saved Khmelnytsky from death.

At the end of December 1647, he departed for the Zaporozhian seich with a small (300–500-man) detachment. There he was elected hetman. This event marked the beginning of a new Kozak uprising, which quickly turned into what might be considered the first modern national revolution.

Khmelnytsky was married three times. His first wife, who was the mother of all his children, died prematurely during the horrors of 1647. His second wife, Matrona, whom he married in early 1649, was the former wife of his enemy D. Czaplinski! In 1651, while Khmelnytsky was away on a military campaign, she was executed for conspiracy and adultery by his son Tymish. In the summer of 1651, Khmelnytsky married Hanna Zolotarenko, a Kozak woman from Korsun and the widow of Col Pylypets. Surviving him by many years, she entered religious service in 1671 and adopted the religious name of Anastasia. Khmelnytsky had two sons and four daughters. His older son, Tymish Khmelnytsky, died on 15 September 1653 in the siege of the Moldavian fortress of Suceava.

The younger son, Yuri Khmelnytsky, was elected during his father's lifetime heir apparent under Ivan Vyhovsky's regency. Yuri twice held the office of hetman.

Khmelnytsky was buried on 25 August 1657 in Saint Elijah's Church in Subotiv, which he himself had built. Khmelnytsky's greatest achievement in the process of national revolution was the Kozak Hetman state of the Zaporozhian Host (1648–1782). His statesmanship was demonstrated in all areas of state-building—in the military, administration, finance, economics, and culture. With political acumen, he invested the Zaporozhian Host under the leadership of its hetman with supreme power in the new Ukrainian state, and unified all the estates of Ukrainian society under his authority. Khmelnytsky built a government system (Khmelnychchyna) and developed military and civilian administrations, which survived in spite of setbacks and difficulties, in the face of Muscovy's invasion, and against Polish and Turkish claims almost to the end of the 18th century.

Kozak Fighting Styles and Tactics

As with any other military elite, there can only be a limited amount definition of specific styles and/or tactics. Because of their very nature, a military elite is flexible, willing and able to absorb new, better systems. During the period of our group's impression, 1648 to 57, there were great changes brought about by the rebellion, so I will divide this period into three sections to better give a more valid interpolation.

The early Kozak Period to the first battles of the rebellion used traditional skills of the Kozaky. These were developed over a period of almost two centuries of constant warfare with the Tatars and Turks invading the Ukraine for slaves and booty. This small scale hit and run warfare honed the personal fighting skills of each seasoned warrior to the utmost. Every Kozak, before venturing into the Wild Lands, would ensure that he was well armed including; a large dagger, saber, and a long distance weapon, either a recurved bow or musquet. The recurved bow was much favored as a noble and effective weapon by the early Kozaky. Indeed bows were still common as late as The Great Northern Wars. The musquet was adopted very quickly by the Kozaky and used to great effect. Until the time of the rebellion, the most common gun would be the matchlock. Some early Kozaky did have wheellock pistols, but due to their cost and complexity they would be rare.

Any Kozak engaged in fighting would rather pick off an opponent at distance with musquet or bow, followed by pistol if available, and then engage with the cold steel of the saber. It is true that as with many warriors based societies, it was considered more noble and valorous to fight hand to hand with saber, but the realities of war are, that it is far better to kill your opponent by the safest and cheapest method possible.

The tactics of this period were dictated by the terrain and enemy, the wide open Steppe and the elusive Tatar, or massed armies of the Turk. The Steppe was a sea of grass mixed with scrub with small areas of forest along rivers or spring areas, much like the land of East Texas. This afforded little cover for large armies, but perfect cover for ambuscade. The Kozaky developed the tabor or wagon train as a method of taking their defensive positions with them. In some cases, these were just typical carts and wagons of the period or they could be heavily armored wagons with protection for the crew with wood and iron boarding for the animals. In the vast Steppe, the Kozak army tended to lure the enemy into attacking the tabor by making short forays and lightning attacks to enrage the enemy into the often fatal move of a direct assault on the tabor, bristling as it was with musquets and small artillery mounted on and/or in the wagons.

Even at this early juncture, one of the most spectacular tactics of the Kozaky had developed. The musquet fire of the Kozaky was famous because of their unique way of producing a remarkable high speed yet accurate storm of lead shot. They accomplished this through a stoic attitude and logical thinking through of the problem of slow loading weapons of the period. All other armies used a fire by rank system, which allowed each musqueteer to fire then return to the rear to reload and step forward by rank to prepare for the next shot. The firelock or matchlock gun of this period was heavy, slow to reload, and dangerous due to constantly lit match, etc. The Kozaky answer to the same problem was totally different, the best marksman stood in

Woodcut by Vasyl Lopata

front of a similar rank system, however, there is where he stayed thanks to a runner standing to his left who took his spent gun back to the rear rank where his gun was reloaded in stages/ranks until it was handed back to him over his right shoulder as he gave the spent gun to the next runner (the person who gave the gun then became the next runner). This gave an unbelievably high rate of fire that was often put down to magic or demonic spells by the terrified enemy! The downside was, of course, the best marksman died first, but constant practice and their stoic belief made sure the front rank was full and effective. One other practice that, though not unique as both the English and Swedes tried it, was the fact that most if not all Kozaky were equipped with a half pike, spear, or at least a sharpened stake to assist in the defense of their block of infantry against enemy cavalry.

If not able to defend or forced to attack, the classic Asian crescent formation was used for the infantry with whatever cavalry was available in the flanks. You will note that the mounted Kozak was rare at this time. The vast majority of Kozaky fought as infantry, indeed most cavalry still preferred to dismount before engaging the enemy.

During the rebellion, many changes happened in the fighting style and tactics of the Kozaky. The enemy changed radically, there had been rebellions before, but now this was a full scale war against the Polish Commonwealth. This meant fighting highly trained cavalry famed for an almost divine strength of attack, fine artillery, and highly trained mercenary infantry. There were also local levies of a significantly lower caliber, but this was an enemy hardened in wars against Sweden, Moscovy, Turks, and Kozaky! However, from the start, the Kozaky army was also different. They now had a vast and highly skilled light cavalry, their old enemy, the Tatar. The treaty that brought the Tatar Khanate to the Kozak side *appeared* to be Bohdan Khmelnitsky's greatest achievement, indeed only the willingness of the Tatars to change sides negated this advantage.

The personal style of fighting would appear to have changed little. Even at the great battles of the rebellion it was common, almost mandatory, for opponents to challenge each other to single combat. Even during the great sieges, single combat and duels were fought on as regular if not almost daily practice. It is worth noting that *both sides* considered themselves knights fighting for "The Cause." One thing that did change was the size of the armies. After Yellow Waters, thousands of serfs, peasants and adventurers joined the ranks of the Kozaky, and thousands of Poles and mercenaries joined the Polish side. Many serfs and peasants joined the Kozak/Rebel army with only hastily converted farm tools, if that. Another great change that came after the first victories was the mounting of thousands of the Kozaky/Rebel army, thanks to the destruction of the Polish armies. The majority still fought dismounted, but more and more skilled cavalry, such as the Registered Kozaky and minor Ruthian gentry, joined the rebellion. The beginnings of the famed Kozaky Cavalry were being formed. A change in personal fighting regretfully starts here also. The way non-combatants are treated becomes a great sorrow, as it does so often in civil wars and revolutions. Both sides are charged with excessive brutality to various sections of the Ukrainian and Polish communities. Mass tortures, rapes, and killings were undoubtedly a part of this rebellion on both sides. It should be noted that the broad sheet (early newspaper) had been born of the horrors of The Thirty Years War and was just coming to age in Eastern Europe, nothing sells like sex and violence. This rebellion had also been used extensively by some political and religious groups to vilify others and promote both period and modern national agendas.

Tactically, another change was that artillery became available in ever greater numbers. The great increase in numbers brought some benefits to the Kozak/Rebel army, but mostly huge logistical and command problems. Sieges, terror, raids, and reprisals in the form of mass executions became common, as did partisan and terrorist warfare. In all, the Modern War was born.

The third and final stage of our period saw extensions of the changes wrought by the rebellion in so far as the continued development and expansion of mounted Kozaky, artillery and peasant armies. There was one regretful change from our Kozaky point of view, more and more there would be battles between Kozak and Kozak, Peasant and Peasant, as the once great rebellion for freedom settled down into internal warfare between Ukrainians and counter rebellions. shifted alliances between the Kozaky and Ukrainians.

The Kozaky at Sea

During the 16th and 17the centuries, the Kozaky became a great maritime power, following in their ancestors, the Viking Russ', footsteps. The catalyst for those seagoing exploits was slavery. By the 1500s, the Turks had forced the Crimean Tatars to recognize Ottoman authority, and were conducting trade in Ukrainian slaves at the Crimean port of Kaffa. Abducted by Tartars during lightning raids on the southern Ukraine, young girls were carried off to become concubines in Turkish harems. Men and boys went directly into the ranks of oarsmen, though the luckier ones became janissaries. So it came to pass that the slave market at Kaffa burned in the hearts of Ukrainians, and especially in those of the Kozaky of the wild empty steppe lands.

Understandably, early Kozak successes gained the attention of the Turks' European enemies. The Papacy, the French and Hapsburg courts opened diplomatic relations with the Kozaky in hopes of launching joint campaigns against the Turks. During one such mission to the Kozaky in June 1594, Hapsburg diplomat Erich von Lasotta recorded in his journal that he arrived in camp just as 1,300 Kozaky under Bohdan Mikosinsky were returning from a successful 50-ship sea raid. From 1600 to 1624, the Zaporozhian sea campaigns reached their greatest magnitude.

During that period, raids involved 40 to 80 shallow draft galleys called chaiky, (pewit, Ukr.) Each longship was up to 60 feet long and 12 feet in both width and depth. Chaiky were made from stone oak, linden, ash or other hardwood trees growing along lower Dnieper. To enhance the chaika's buoyancy, sheaves of reeds were fastened along both sides to act as a flotation collar. They also provided some protection against enemy cannon fire. The longships were

Unknown Artist

propelled by 10 to 12 sets of oars, and one or two square-rigged sails. The masts were lowered before going into battle, making the vessel almost invisible at a distance. Chaika also featured rudders located at both the bow and stern, providing exceptional mobility. A chaika could execute a 180-degree turn within its own length. The main armament consisted of up to eight falkonetts, which were augmented by the muskets and sabers that each crew member carried. Blunderbusses/horse guns were very popular for boarding enemy vessels and close-quarter combat because of their wider shot pattern. Each galley was equipped with its own compass, not the norm for such small vessels in the 17th century.

The Kozak chaika was often augmented by a number of Turkish-style galleys that served as command-and-control ships for the senior officers. These larger vessels were powered by about 30 oars, and three or four sails. They also mounted larger cannons than the chaiky. A distinctive feature of these vessels was the mast arrangement, the foremast was the tallest of the three, the mainmast the shortest.

Petro Konashevych Sahaidachny was elected hetman in 1613. Sahaidachny was a dynamic nobleman from the Halychyna region of the western Ukraine. After studying at the Ostrih Academy, he quickly rose in the ranks and helped lead successful raids against several Turkish strongholds along the western shore of the Black Sea, including Varna (1606), Ochakiv (1607), Perekop (1607 and 1608), Kilia (1609), Ismail (1609) and Akkerman (1609).

It has been said that Sahaidachny realized that the Zaporozhian host could be the start of a Ukrainian nation. By attacking Ottoman targets, he hoped to obtain recognition and support from the European states opposing the Turks in the Balkans and Eastern Europe. By 1618, the Zaporozhians were members of the Imperialist Anti-Turkish League. Sahaidachny even moved the official leader's seat of power to the old Ukrainian capital of Kyiv (Kiev), and conducted a foreign policy that was nominally under the Polish Crown's authority, but for practical purposes was independent.

In the early summer of 1614, 40 vessels and 2,000 men headed for the Anatolian coast. The towns and cities on its shoreline made up a 17th-century Turkish Riviera, populated by rich merchants. Leaving two men behind per ship to guard the fleet, Sahaidachny and the Kozaky proceeded to plunder and sack their first landfall, Trebizond. From there, they used former slaves as guides to make a surprise attack on the luxurious Anatolian pleasure port of Sinope, known in the Ottoman Empire as the "City of Lovers." Storming the port from the landward side, the Kozaky seized the citadel, and in addition to sacking the city, destroyed the large Turkish fleet of galleys and galleons at anchor in the harbor. In 1615, one of the great Kozaky naval exploits came to pass. After entering the Bosporus, an 80-vessel fleet landed the Kozaky between Mizevna and Archioca, the twin ports of Constantinople. Sahaidachny split his forces into two units, which simultaneously assaulted and plundered both ports. According to the Ottoman chronicles, Sultan Ahmed I saw the smoke from the burning ports while on a hunting trip and immediately ordered the janissaries from the 30,000-man garrison to engage and massacre the Kozaky; however, Sahaidachny quickly recalled the Kozaky, who re-embarked before the janissaries arrived. After a four-day pursuit along the west coast of the Black Sea, the Turks overtook the Kozaky near the mouth of the Danube. At that point, the Kozaky, making use of the chaika's superior mobility, suddenly reversed course and attacked the leading Turkish galleys, capturing the Turkish admiral! With the loss of their commander, Turkish morale collapsed and their remaining vessels fled southward. The Kozaky, in a typical gesture of defiance, towed the captured galleys to Ochakiv and burned them in view of its garrison. Using the burning vessels as a diversion, some of the Kozaky slipped ashore, seized all the garrison's cattle and horses, and drove them overland to the Sich.

After returning to camp, each man received his fair portion of the spoils and hid it in a secret underwater location along the labyrinth of small islands, reed beds and marshes. As a result, this region of the Dnieper became known as Shcharbniza Voyskova, or "Treasury of the Kozaky."

A modern representation of a heavy chaika in battle
By the artist Dan Horsechief

The Kozak naval raids finally petered out, because they found more lucrative markets for their talents during the Thirty Years' War. Kozaky fought first for the Hapsburgs, and later for France. There was even one regiment of Kozaky who fought in their Chaika in the **Baltic** against the Swedes for the Poles with some good measure of success! By the end of these wars, the rebellion of 1648 had taken root. There were engagements throughout the region by river, both attacking Polish supply vessels and in siege actions.

One unusual weapon of the seaborne Kozaky was the fire tube. This was a pointed copper or brass tube filled with an explosive warhead, a considerable amount of powdered propellant and a short fuse that was launched from the small shipboard cannon on the chaika as an incendiary device. It seems that a short length chain trailed behind as a stabilizer and to ensure attachment to the rigging of the opponent's ship.

Mention must be made of the legend of the undersea Chaika. These craft appear in more than one folk tale regarding the attacks on Turkish cities. The vague descriptions vary from what may have been merely an upturned and weighted small boat to a true underwater craft. These descriptions convey a craft powered by rear or side mounted jointed oars and raised and lowered by compression of goatskin bladders. Perhaps, an archeological discovery will one day give another first to the Kozaky!

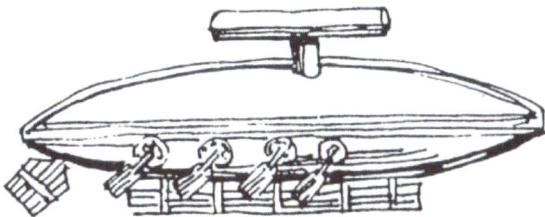

A period drawing of a more advanced form of underwater Chaika that appears to be very similar to Dutch designs of the period.

Kozaky Drink

There are no known records of the first ice distillation, as this may have happened almost as soon as wine or beer was made in the North. However, it is known that the first heat distilled alcohol probably reached Poland from the German states in the 15th century, and it is recorded that the term 'wodka' was known from at least 1534. The first recorded distillery was established in the Baltic city of Danzig by a Dutchman in the 16th century. While in Baltic Estonia, written records indicate the distillation of alcohol in 1485. Heat distilled alcohol reached Ukraine about the same time. The first recorded distilleries were in Sokal, Hrabivec, and Tushivci. From these western towns, they spread east. In Poland, the term Gorzale wino (for a triple distilled alcohol) was shortened to 'gorzalka', which was rendered into Ukrainian as *horilka* , which is still the standard term.

It has been noted in several period accounts, that most horilka was already flavored, or more correctly, drugged. Common additives include St. Johns Wort, bison grass, hemp, and saltpeter. These special versions are now thought to have helped control the Sich Kozaky. It is known that there was an immediate and total ban on drinking following the start of war maneuvers, being cut off "Cold Turkey" would have caused serious mental changes in the Sich warriors. As most of the common additives have calming and sexual represent effects, these changes would have all been beneficial in stirring the men forward to war.

The traditional non-distilled beverages in Ukraine include *med* , or mead. This most ancient of drinks did not have the same popularity after the introduction of *horilka* in Poland, but it was still much drank. Beers included *pyvo*, a hopped beer, *braha,* an unhopped millet beer, and *kvas,* a generic name for a wide variety of fermented beverages, from fruits, berries and beets, and bread. Beyond these, there are two rather unusual beers. *Berezovyj,* which is made from fermented birch sap, and *klenovyj sik,* from fermented maple sap! In many period sources, the conjoined word *med-pyvo*, or mead-beer appears, and denoted an abundance of different alcoholic beverages that were a mix of one or more of these types.

The term *vyno* (wine) was used for imported grape wine, and being imported, only the affluent could afford it.

An excellent representation of Kozaky Kortchuma (inn)
Artist: Victor Macklok

Козаку Food

Ukrainian Kozaky food of the mid-seventeenth century already included influences from a great many different cultures. Polish food had a great influence of course, but there are distinct Turkish/Tatar influences (themselves influenced by both Arabic and Greek cuisine), and Muscovite. Some Western European influences can also be detected. The exact date of when the first foods from the Americas arrived, probably via Arabic or Armenian traders (although trade with the West was also very strong) are hotly debated. The best solution for valid living historical recreations of our period is, if it comes from the Americas, ***do not use it***!

Typical Kozaky fare needs to be broken down into two distinct types for reenactment purposes, campaign and Sich food. The fine home and *Kortchuma* food would constitute too vast an area to do it justice. I suggest you purchase a good Ukrainian cookbook and bear in mind the note above on food from the Americas.

Campaign Food

Gruel is the simple answer, gruel and more gruel! Kozaky gruel, called *Teteria*, was traditionally made from millet, buckwheat, rye, and/or wheat in any combination or mix. This was flavored with salt or more rarely, honey or maple syrup. There is occasional mention of meat or fat added as in Western Europe, but this seems rarer. If there was meat available from a hunting party or raid, this would be first roasted on an open fire. The leftovers would be used to make the famed *Vareniky*, or dumplings, like pierogies, or ravioli. These *Vareniky* were the favorite food of the Kozaky, and the ability to make good ones was an art well prized amongst the warriors. They can be stuffed with cheese, fruit, meat, fish, or a surprising mixture of the above. Another variation is the *Halushky*, another dumpling more like the German or Jewish type, where the flavoring is mixed into the dumpling, not filled into a center.

Beyond these favorites, bread and cheeses would have been commonly eaten along with sausages. This simple fare would have been expanded from raids, depending on where and whom the Kozaky were fighting. Their foods would have suddenly included Polish sausages and sauerkraut to fine lamb in basil with a turmeric sauce and Turkish delight!

Simple foraging would have also brought in wild fruits, berries, wild game, and any unfortunate domesticated animals within reach of the troop!

Remember, no strong drinks were allowed on campaign for the Sich Kozaky, but they would not have been so foolish to drink water! They would have drank *pyvo*, a hopped beer, *braha* an un-hopped millet beer, and *kvas* the light fermented drink made from fruit, beets or bread for safety. They may not have understood the biology of impure water, but they would have been all too aware of the concrescences.

The Sich

The food of the Kozaky at the Sich was basically similar to campaign food, with the addition of soups (more like our stews in their heavy content). Most famous was the great Ukrainian *Borsch*! There is no one recipe for this National dish, for there are regional and family versions. It always has beets and usually cabbage; however, beyond this it can be with meat or fish, etc. Hard boiled eggs, cucumbers, mushrooms, and sour cream make up a regular secondary list of ingredients.

Each *Kurin* or section of the Sich took turns fishing and hunting in prescribed areas to bring in fresh food. The great river supplied a variety of fish for drying and the famed giant crayfish, which were one of the symbols of the *Zaporózhtzi*. The fish, either dried or fresh, often ended up in a cabbage, onion, and fish soup that marked another famed Sich dish, *Scherba*.

The hunted wild game was also dried later in the year, but could also become a roast for special occasions. These roasts would often be marinated in a mix of herbs and fruits that give a sweet and savory flavor we now call bar-b-que. These would be served with a range of breads.

Beyond the gruels of the campaigns, there was a great range of healthy grain dishes often called *Kashas,* and the great Polish/Ukrainian dish Plohv, a pilaf of grains, pasta, fruits and meats that show a strong Eastern influence.

Many types of bread were also baked within the Sich and the surrounding ring of stall holders, who risked the wrath of the Kozaky for their wealth. These merchants also sold just about every kind of food and drink that might interest a Kozak.

The vegetables used included of course beets, onions, scallions, celery like stalks, cucumbers, cabbages, both red and green, (it should be noted that the cabbages of the period are more like Chinese cabbage), parsley root and leaves. Kholodets, a Ukrainian aspic dish, could include meat, vegetable, or even sweet additions such as mint and honey.

Do not forget hard boiled eggs. These appear in so many dishes from salads to soups, sauces and pickled. Finally, mention must be made of the fruits of the Sich; these were far more common than might be expected. Melons were much cultivated, even within the Sich itself; however, the most used fruit by far was the famed Ukrainian cherry!

Another excellent representation of Kozaky Kortchuma (inn)
Artist: Victor Macklok

An Introduction to Kozaky Medicine

Kozaky medicine must be broken down into distinct sections, as with food, because the situation would greatly determine type of medicine employed by the Kozaky. As has already been mentioned in the section on Kozaky drink, the Kozaky society was well versed in the use of drugs and how to use them, both chronically and in an emergency.

Medicine at war: The first medical application for any wound was to clean the wound out with horilka, and then sprinkle gun powder on the wound and set light to the powder. Chewed bread and/or spider's web was placed in the wound prior to bandaging. This is a very effective cleansing and healing regimen. This was often followed by the internal consumption of gun powder. This, however, would have little effect except to reduce sexual appetite and function, perhaps a good thing if severely wounded. Certain highly acidic mosses were often put under the bandage to absorb fluids and act as a barrier to infection.

Pain reducing medications were well known and used, including an aspirin product derived from willow bark, hemp, and opium. There were other herbs used for both internal and external pain reduction.

Kozaky medical station in battle
Artist unknown

Medicine at the Sich: expanded in the range of herbs available and the persons able to treat wounds, or now, illness. The Sich and its surrounding town of merchants could provide medicines and styles of medicine from most of the world. Many Armenian, Turkish and Arabic doctors plied their trade here along with the inevitable quacks and charlatans.

Medicine at the Zymivnyk: Healing suddenly changes from the all male world of war and the Sich to being in the hands of the women folk. The most qualified amongst them would be known as **Mudra Zhiulna**, wise/holy mother, and medicine now merges with faith. As with most peoples of the world at this time, the line between medicine and magic is vague at best and often indistinguishable. This does not in anyway mean that it was less effective, indeed, the scientifically verified effect of placebo effect can be very positive (not to take anything away from faith based healing). Some of the powerful herbal mixes for salves, infusions and aromatics have survived through historical times and appear to have valid medicinal value.

Unfortunately, due to the dangerous nature of many ingredients used, we can not expound upon them! What can be said is that many modern herbals containing teas, salves, and the like would have been used in our time. For specific information on a practice or concoction you may contact our own Mudra Zhiulna, Zobiana…

The Kozak Religious Concept

The traditional Kozak stereotype is of an ignorant Eastern Orthodox bigot who murders Jews on sight. This, like *all* stereotypes, *is a ridiculous oversimplification* that does not even scratch the surface of the Kozak religious concept. It continues to pervade some "Histories" because it carries a strong propaganda message that is of use to some countries and policies.

The Kozaky were made up of many eastern European (Ukrainian, Ruthian, Lithuanian, Prussian, etc.) peoples, mainly of the peasant and poorer landed classes with the odd fleeing noble. These were areas that had either fairly recently had Christianity thrust upon by extreme force, as in Prussia, or by the upper classes in Ruthia, or in the case of Lithuania, only in a very limited and superficial way. As in most cases of mass conversion, either forced or not, the people of the land tended to keep to their traditional earth and fertility centered ways to some extent. This seems to be very evident amongst the Kozaky. You will note that the questioning of the incoming Kozak still contains Earth Mother orientated wording, and is typical of dual faith oaths of Europe. In fact, the term Dual Faith was coined to cover Ruthian/Russian peasants in the 19th century when most still held Earth centered beliefs.

It has been noted that the Rada was held around a "Sacred Oak" and this tree was decorated in spring. Kozaky were also known in folklore as sorcerers, and called in to bury sorcerers in other areas. There is folklore myth that the first Kozaky were "Forest Men" or outlaws living in the forests around Kiev. These men were known as *Kiys*, "The Men of the Spear," (*Kiyki* is spear in old Ukrainian) and had been brought beyond the rapids by a prince to fight the Tatar.

During the early rebellions, agents of Muscovy (and Sweden) often used the Jewish leaseholder as a scapegoat. Some Eastern Orthodox priests working in cooperation with Muscovite agents

Rendition of a classic Ukrainian place of worship
Artist: Unknown

developed the propaganda of Kozaky oppression as being the Catholics, especially the Jesuit priests working in league with the Jews.

By the time of the Khmelnitsky rebellion, many (if not most) Kozaky had become converted to Orthodoxy, at least to some extent. The conversions would appear to be less definite the further East and North the Kurin. Kurins and Kozak villages outside of the Sich are known to have carried on the tradition of the Kolduna, Mudra Zhiulna and other shamanistic practices well into the 20th century. The true religious view of the Kozaky *may* be summed up in the following prayer; originally offered up to Zorya/Lada, the virgin Goddess, and companion to Perun/Yor, the ancient Russ/Kozaky God of War (very similar to the Nordic Thor or Germanic Donar). Later another Virgin may well have been intended.

O Virgin, unsheathe your father's sacred sword.
Take up the breastplate of your ancestors.
Take up your powerful helmet.
Bring forth your steed of black
Fly to the open field, there the great army with countless weapons is found.
O Virgin, cover me with your veil.
Protect me against the power of the enemy, against gun and arrow, warriors and weapons,
Be they of wood, bone, copper, lead, iron or steel.

The Kozaky Spirit World

This section covers a different concept from the previous religion section in that this covers a basic, and in many ways deeper, world view of the Kozaky and their fellow dwellers in the Wild Fields and beyond. The Ukrainian reverence for nature and the intertwined world of the Nature Spirits was, and is still to a very great extent, part of the true Ukrainian psyche.

Each geographic area of Kozaky life would be governed by a spirit of some form from the hearth, home, forests, or river, to vast plains of the wild fields. These spirit forms were natural and as real a part of the scenery as any rock or tree. Each had a name and a way of interacting with our human world. More importantly, each spirit could be angered or placated by human interaction with their natural world. The following paragraphs will cover each area a Kozaky might travel through and the Nature Spirits to be aware of in the respective abodes.

Every house, including the Kurin, is home to a Domovoi and his wife, most likely a Domania or Kikimora. These spirits of the hearth and home were very important to the wellbeing of the inhabitants. A small part of each meal or bread and salt would be regularly left out for them. The Domovoi may take on the appearance of the elder of the household, causing some confusion and eventually consternation after the death of the elder. The Domania would not tolerate a messy home and would wake children and others at night by tickling and making strange noises to make her feeling known. Often, she would also take on the appearance of the elder lady of the home, but would always have her hair down (unlike Ukrainian wives). These spirits are of great use to the home/Kurin as they help keep things in order, and more importantly, will howl or moan if danger approaches. They will also warn a woman by pulling her hair if there is danger to her.

In the yard, the spirit is generally known as a Dvorovoi and these can be quite a handful. They hate white animals, except chickens (because of the divine nature of the egg), but once again can be placated small gifts of food and shiny gifts. Further on in the barn dwells the Ovinnik, often appearing as a large wild cat that needs to be kept happy with pancakes or it might set fire to the barn with its red burning eyes.

The last of the Home Spirits is the Bannik. Living in the bathhouse, he is the most powerful of these home centered spirits. Once again, he will often appear as a familiar person. The bath house was the last stronghold of the Pagan past (and the first place of its return). Christian icons never appeared here. Even in strongly Orthodox families, this was the place of older symbols of the Moist Mother Earth, a place for birthing of children, and ritual or everyday cleansing.

Kozak and Mudra Zhiulna
Artist: A. Bazylevych

As we move beyond the confines of the home, we must deal with the one all-pervading spirit of all the Slavic lands, the Moist Mother Earth, Mati-Syra-Zemlya, or Mokosh. In reality, the ancient dark Earth Mother never left the people through successive waves of religion. Later she would become St. Paraskeva, but never change or leave the dark Ukrainian soil. The earth would never be abused. Children are told not to poke her with sticks. Oaths made holy by the earth included the Kozaky oath. There is an old Kozak tradition of lifting the soil and putting ones ear to the ground, not only to hear distant horses, but to hear the Moist Mother Earth tell him what he needed to know to protect her.

On the great steppe of the Wild Fields, as at sea, the winds were a strong friend or foe. Greatest of these is Horishniak, the North Wind. There is also Dogoda, the gentle West wind. Across these steppes were many ancient burial mounds left by various races across the vast expanse of time. These were both welcome signposts and still sacred rest stops. However, they are also the haunts of strange and deadly spirits, such as the Vampyr or vampire. This is not the newer western version, the original was a much darker Slavic undead creature that fed on the flesh and blood of the living. The methodology of dispatching these is traditional, an Ash or Birch stake through the heart, followed by beheading. There are also werewolves, Volkodlak, (Ukr.) here, humans, able to take on the attributes and sometimes shape of the wolf. These creatures are usually seen as protectors of the common people that fought evil sorcerers for the safety of crops, forests and ancient places.

On into the woods that fill the gorges and surround the rivers of the Wild Fields, we find the Leshy, the lord and guardian of the forest. He may be in the company of his wife, the Leshachika, and his children, Leshonki. These protectors of the forest and forest folk, such as the bear and wolf, will protect other outcasts of human society, such as bandits and rebels, but will kill those that threaten the forest, such as landlords, loggers and the like.

Rusalka Artist: Unknown

Another spirit of both the forest and the river is the famed Rusalka. These beautiful female spirits live in the forests by summer, rivers by fall, and winter garbed in only a chemise with leaves in their hair garlanded by flowers. As with many female fairy folk, they are both sensual and highly sexual by nature, taking human lovers who may disappear for long periods of times into their world. They help with the creative forces and often invited to feasts with ritual dinners and beer followed by songs and dances. After this play, the young would often frolic in the river naked. This type of celebration reminds one of the greatest of all Kozaky feasts, Kupalo's eve (June 21st) and later, St. John's Eve (either June 21st or 24th). All these feasts and rites show how the ancient and the new coexisted more openly in the East than in Western Europe.

The Orthodox church, allowed the Nature Spirits to live on, not driving them away as demons of Western Christianity, and their followers were not branded as evil. Thus, the terrible witch trials of the West did not plague Eastern Europe to the extent that they did in the West.

The Kozaky lived in a harsh warrior's world, fighting constantly against the true evil of slavery by Turk and Tatar, and against serfdom of the Polish magnate. Yet, it was also imbued with the wonder and sacredness of life and nature all around them.

Addendum 1

A Rough Guide to Obtaining Authentic Kosak Equipment

The best way to cure a problem is to stop it before it starts… This guide to suppliers should help you get the right items at a fair price. Although this is updated regularly, some suppliers may no longer trade or sell a particular item (please feel free to contact me with better/newer information). Here then is what I have found, so far, in the same order as the Kosaky Handbook:

Swords, Sabers and Main Gauche/Daggers: For rapiers, I strongly suggest the Paul Chen Practical range. These are often cheapest from E-Bay, but check with By-the-Sword too. For sabres the only weapon I can personally vouch for is the Museum Replica's Scimitar.

Armor and Helmets: Helmets are not really applicable to Kozaky. As for armor, chain can be worn under garments if you wish. There is no reliable source for authentic chain, except Museum Replica's rather high priced items. So, check E-bay and take your choice.

Fire Arms: Heritage Arms has an excellent matchlock long gun. They also have doglock long guns and pistols. As this is a really big ticket item, please check before you buy!

Men's Footwear: The best and absolutely correct boot comes from Arm Streets Old Ways (an E-Bay store) the lower point toe boot is perfect and a good value at about $160. A cheaper, but authentic option would be from Medieval Moccasins for Kozak Postoly.

Men's Trousers: I suggest you make your own, but the standard draw string trouser from Chivalry Sports or Museum Replicas will do just fine.

Men's Shirts: Again, I suggest you make your own. Please *beware* of "Ukrainian" shirts with "traditional" folk embroidery, a **very few** amongst officers is OK, but they are very rare in our time. DO NOT BUY THEM!

Men's Zhupán and Kontuse Coats: The best Zhupán money can buy, as long as you are not over 42" chest, is from Museum Replicas. For larger sizes and specials, you need The Polish Hussar Plus online store (as above).

Sabre Belts, etc. For all specials you need The Polish Hussar Plus online store (**www.polishhussarsupply.com**) Just tell them who you are with and confirm you period impression – Ukrainian Kozak of the Rebellion Period – **and he will keep you straight on everything**. One other place to look is **www.ataman.com.ua,** they have a lot of very good items, goat whips, hats, etc. However, be careful of a lot of NON-PERIOD items, as ever, ask first!

Addendum 2
Kozak Wars on a Smaller Scale

Another area of interest to many of the Kozaky groups is wargames and role-playing of our period. Why should adults with an expensive and invigorating hobby need to play with "toy soldiers"? The answer has a lot to do with living history and getting to know our period. We can not (not for the time being anyway!) field an army of over a hundred infantry, equal numbers of cavalry, and large artillery, supported by a baggage train; yet this is relatively inexpensive and easily co-coordinated on the wargame table. This advantage in numbers and types of troops available really does give another perspective on our times. Plus there are times that we can not be out there on the field, and you just do not want to repair another piece of equipment or polish your sabre again!

What is a wargame? It is a military action in miniature, guided by rules set down to give an accurate impression of the interaction of troops during battle including; tactics, rate of fire, moral, casualties, and movement. The rules are generally fairly simple to allow the action to flow at a reasonable and enjoyable rate.

What is role-playing? It is similar to the above description, but focusing on the individual and their strengths and weaknesses, usually involving fewer figures. The two can be rolled into one to produce a smaller tactical level scenario, such as portrayed by the rules for *Kozak Wars*.

All figures painted by the Author

Scale is a serious consideration in wargames, as the figures vary in size from 5mm to 30mm in height. The obvious differences are the amount of detail vs. size of army portrayed. Due to the smaller numbers involved in role-playing, the normal scale used is 25-30mm.

Figures:

In the original Kozaky group, the decision was made, mainly because of existing armies and quality of available figures, to adopt the classic 25-28 mm scale as the standard for the group.

The best figures available in this scale for the Kozak Wars Period include:
Assault Group Renaissance Cossacks (10 sets) *My NEW personal favorite, there is a figure of Maks (the Author in the Cossack General set!*
All 28mm great period feel perfect for rebellion period, if a bit pricey.
Old Glory **Cossack Wars** (17 sets)
Old Glory Ottoman Turks (43 sets)
Old Glory Eastern Renaissance Armies (43 sets)
Old Glory Revolting Mob (6 sets)
There are also yurts, Slavic fortifications and an excellent Ukrainian farmstead.
*These are fairly inexpensive, have very good detail, and with a few exceptions, provide accurate representations of our period troops and equipment. (25mm **Cossack Wars** sets nearer 28mm*
Foundry Kozaky (8 sets)
More expensive, but very well detailed and executed miniatures (28mm)
Essex Miniatures
Muscovite (16 figures)
Kozak (12 figures)
Polish (24 figures)
Tartars (4 figures)
Good traditional wargame quality figures (20-25mm)
Redoubt Enterprises
Renaissance Infantry, Cavalry, and Artillery (about 40 sets)
Good quality figures, some oddities (25mm).

One important thing for any set of figures to make them usable in conjunction with each other, for any set of rules, is the bases. In order to keep an optimal ability to use various rules (and costs down), we use the traditional wooden 3" by 1 ½" base available from Wal-Mart in the craft section. Figures are mounted in pairs (or singly) for infantry and as a single for cavalry.

Rules:

Some of the most popular for our period and area of interest are:

Kozak Wars – Wargaming in the age of the Kozaky by Stephen Lawrence
A good mix of small skirmish action and a hint of role-playing that can be adapted to our needs. About $20.00 (often much cheaper on E-Bay)

Lion of the North 2 – Haiduk and Rajtar by Michael Peters
A classic wargames rule set developed for the mid seventeenth century and very good for larger battles. Free on the web.

Friekorps - by Bryan Ansell of Guernsey Foundry. A great skirmish level set of rules. Free on the web.

Pick a Side!

The last consideration for entering into wargames of our period will be picking a side. This may be a forgone conclusion for many due to personal heritage, deeply held convictions, etc. It may be worth a few moments of consideration. There is often nothing more fun and interesting than representing "*the other side*". This holds true in full scale reenacting as in wargames (e.g. Maks' infamous rendition of Mathew Hopkins, the "Witch-finder General"!). So, just think about being a greedy Tartar, merciless Polish magnate or "loyal registered Kozak" before you dash off to set up as your first thought. One last thought, there is nothing wrong with an all Kozak wargame table. *Unfortunately,* the Kozaky history is full of counter rebellions and straight out tribal warfare.

THE END...

Well not quite the end... The Partial Bibliography

This work has been a long time in coming, but I really need to give credit where credit is due, for this has been a long labor of love and so many passages from books, web sites, etc., helping to formulate this booklet. I hereby offer my humble apologies to all those I may have missed. It has not been done on purpose, I assure you, merely memory fails where I picked up a piece of information.

Peoples Memory of Cossacks
A. Gaidai, S P Interbook of Zaporozhye, Ukraine. 1991

A Description of Ukraine
Guillaume Le Vasseur, Sieur de Beauplan – Translated by A. Pernal & D. Essar
Harvard Ukrainian Research Institute, Cambridge MA, USA 1993

Hryhorij Hrabjank's The Great War of Bohdan Xmel'nyc'kyj
Edited and introduction by Dr. Yuri Lutsenko, Harvard Ukrainian Research Institute, Cambridge MA, USA 1990

The Cossack and Religion in Early Modern Ukraine
Serhii Plokhy, Oxford University Press, GB 2001

Cossacks of the Brotherhood, The Zaporog Kosh of the Dnieper River
G. Patrick Marsh, Peter Lang Publishing of New York, USA. 1990

An Introduction to Ukrainian History Volume 2
Nicholas Chirovsky, Philosophical Library, Inc. of New York, USA. 1984

Polish Armies 1596-1696 2 Men-At-Arms Series # 188
Richard Brezezinski Angus McBride, Osprey – Reed Consumer Books, GB. 1988

Between Remembrance and Denial
Joel Raba, East European Monographs of Boulder, USA 1995

Cossack - *Warrior Riders of the Steppes*
M.A. Groushko, Sterling Pub Co Inc, USA 1993

A Course in Russian History – The Seventeenth Century
V. O. Kliuchevsky – Translated by Natalie Duddington, ME Sharpe of London, England 1993

The Time of Troubles
S. F. Platonov –Translated by John T. Alexander, University Press of Kansas 1986

The Disturbed State of the Russian Realm
Conrad Busslow – Translated by G Edward Orchard, McGil-Queens University Press of London, England 1994

History of the Cossacks
Gen. Wasili G. Glaskow, Roberts Speller and Sons, New York, USA1972

Slavic Sorcery
Kenneth Johnson, Llewellyn Publications of St. Paul, USA 1998

The *Bath House at Midnight, Magic in Russia*
W. F. Ryan, The Pennsylvania University Press of University Park, USA 1999

Songs of the Russian People as illustrative of Slavic Mythology and Russian Life
W. R. S. Ralston. Kessinger Publications, USA (modern reprint of 1872 edition)

Ukrainian Mythology
Valery Vojtovych, Lybid, Kyiv, Ukraine 2005

Down Singing the Centuries, Folk Literature of the Ukraine
Louisa Loeb, translated by F. R. Livesay. Hyperion Press Ltd. Canada 1981

The Best of Ukrainian Cuisine
Bohdan Zahny, Hippocrene Books of New York, USA 1998

For further period, if fictional reading, I can not recommend to highly:
With Fire and Sword
Henryk Sienkiewicz ("in modern translation by W. S. Kuniczak"), Hippocrene Books of New York, USA 1991

Blood Brothers
Vasyl Shevchuck, translated by Yuri Tkach, Bayda Books, Doncaster , Aus. 1980

Taras Bulba
N. Gogol, translated byO. A. Gorhakov, Foreign Languages Publishing House, Moscow, USRR (beware of recent inaccurate translations!)

These three books will give the re-enactor a better "feel" for the Kozak and his world than any others that I *personally* know of.

CPSIA information can be obtained
at www.ICGtesting.com
Printed in the USA
LVHW070735280322
714569LV00002B/18